AN UNOFFICIAL
FAN JOURNAL

I ♥ BTS

**Obsess Over Your Biases, Learn
More about the Bangtan Boys, &**
*CELEBRATE WHAT
IT MEANS TO BE
ARMY!*

YERIN KIM

ADAMS MEDIA
New York London Toronto Sydney New Delhi

Aadamsmedia

Adams Media
An Imprint of Simon & Schuster, Inc.
100 Technology Center Drive
Stoughton, Massachusetts 02072

First Adams Media hardcover edition May 2023

ADAMS MEDIA and colophon are trademarks of
Simon & Schuster.

For information about special discounts for bulk purchases,
please contact Simon & Schuster Special Sales at
1-866-506-1949 or business@simonandschuster.com.

The Simon & Schuster Speakers Bureau can bring authors
to your live event. For more information or to book an event,
contact the Simon & Schuster Speakers Bureau at
1-866-248-3049 or visit our website at
www.simonspeakers.com.

Interior design by Priscilla Yuen
Illustrations by Indira Yuniarti
Interior images © 123RF/archnoi1, rawpixel;
Simon & Schuster, Inc.

Manufactured in the United States of America
Printed by Versa Press Inc., East Peoria, IL, USA

10 9 8 7 6 5 4 3 2 1

ISBN 978-1-5072-2044-3

CONTENTS

INTRODUCTION

When did you realize you were part of ARMY?

Was it when you saw one of the band's music videos for the first time? Could you not get the catchy yet deep lyrics of a particular song out of your head? Or could it have been the first time you felt your heart skip a beat for your bias?

BTS's debut in 2013 skyrocketed them to success! Your favorite band (and mine) has redefined K-pop, created iconic bops, and broken records over and over—and you and ARMY have been there every step of the way!

I Love BTS reintroduces you to your favorite band and lets your imagination run wild. Its members make BTS beyond perfect!

JIN *A foodie, former wannabe actor, and the oldest of the group.*

SUGA *An introverted, silly rapper with a vulnerable side.*

J-HOPE *A fashion-forward dance expert and all-around sweetheart.*

RM *An amazing rapper, leader of the group, and the glue that holds BTS together.*

JIMIN *A sensitive and caring dancer, vocalist, and social media sensation.*

V *A country-grown powerhouse vocalist, photographer, and (even) talented actor.*

JUNGKOOK *The youngest, adorably shy, and a jack-of-all-trades!*

BTS is beyond talented (obviously!), but what we love most about BTS are their unique personalities and the way they connect with each other and their fans. With silly nicknames like "Worldwide Handsome" and adorable moments of *aegyo*, it's impossible to not be a fan of the Bangtan Boys.

As you stream, support, and follow BTS on the daily, use this interactive journal filled with fun prompts. While the whole world knows BTS, only you know exactly what BTS means to you. Here, you'll take your fandom to the next level and dive deep into all the ways the group has changed your life. You'll be able to:

- *Imagine interactions with members by using prompts like "If you could confide in one of the boys, which member would you trust the most with your biggest secret?"*

- *Write about your favorite lyrics with questions about picking your top five lyrics related to love.*

- *Journal about what's next for your favorite band with hypotheticals like "Whether a K-drama appearance, new TV show, or collaboration with a Western musician, what are your dream projects for each member?"*

Not only do you get fun prompts; this journal also tests your fan knowledge! You'll find more than thirty trivia questions on a huge range of topics, challenging even the most devoted fan. In the back of the journal, there's also a place for your own BTS scrapbook. Paste all the cutest, silliest photos of the band (or your bias!), and make this journal your most treasured keepsake. For the band that lives rent-free in your mind, it's time to celebrate the most iconic idols in the world and every reason you love them with *I Love BTS*!

Today, BTS is known as a worldwide sensation that has forever transformed the music industry. But back in 2010, they were just getting started as K-pop trainees. While we know BTS officially debuted in 2013, their story actually began a few years prior, when Big Hit Entertainment (now called HYBE) discovered the boys and their jaw-dropping talents through auditions, competition shows, and scouts. After intense recruiting and a brutal trainee process, the idol group was finalized as the absolutely adorable septet we know and love today, featuring leader RM and members Jungkook, Jimin, V, J-Hope, Suga, and Jin. Originally meant to be a hip-hop group, the boys were rebranded as a more well-rounded idol group to set them up for commercial success. And we're grateful for the change, as it allows our biases the chance to uniquely shine! After toying with names like Big Kids and Young Nation, lucky for us, they ultimately landed on *Bangtan Sonyeondan*—which translates to "Bulletproof Boy Scouts." While definitely a catchy name, the meaning behind it is special. The boys wanted *bangtan*, or "bulletproof," to represent their resistance to the unrealistic stereotypes and expectations that are usually put on young people, especially in Korea. Later, in 2017, the group extended BTS's meaning as part of its rebrand, announcing it would also stand for "Beyond the Scene."

The Bangtan Boys officially entered the scene in 2013, wowing everyone with the album *2 Cool 4 Skool* and its lead single, "No More Dream." Our boys were honored as Best New Artist later that year at the Melon Music Awards, a major award show in the Korean music industry. From the very beginning, they weren't afraid to tackle societal or political issues and personal stories in their music. In fact, "No More Dream" is said to be a commentary on Korea's obsession with education, encouraging listeners to rebel against society's strict expectations and follow their dreams. The boys are super-passionate about conveying important messages through their lyrics. RM has even consulted a regional women's studies professor to make sure their lyrics were sensitive to gender equality. The group also produced much of their own music. Their first full studio album, *Dark & Wild*, became a hit in August 2014, launching their first-ever global concert tour.

After crossing off a series of impressive firsts in Korea, BTS started gaining new international fans, namely in Japan. They eventually came out with a Japanese studio album, *Wake Up*, and went on to tour all over Japan. Since then, BTS have released four more Japanese-language albums as well as many Japanese versions of their Korean tracks. BTS, and mainly V, are so popular in Japan that the country has been nicknamed "TaeTae Land" (for V's real name, Kim Tae-hyung) by fans.

In 2015, the group kicked off a new era with *The Most Beautiful Moment in Life, Pt. 1*, leading with "I Need U." The album traded their dark visuals and hip-hop sound for more reflective lyrics and a pop vibe and proved BTS's incredible musical range and growth since their debut. *Wings* followed in 2016 and immediately climbed up the charts, even breaking Korean album chart records. Most of *Wings*'s track list is actually cowritten by the members of BTS!

Can you believe BTS didn't take off globally until a few years into their career? The year 2017 was a pivotal one for the group. First, they released *Love Yourself: Her*, which RM once described as "the beginning of [their] chapter two." It was instantly a smash hit and the highest-charting Korean album to break into the *Billboard* 200 albums chart. As they gained steam and started to make it big in America, the group truly reached global stardom. They released an all-English song collaboration, "Waste It on Me," with DJ and producer Steve Aoki. Following a win at the Billboard Music Awards, they sang "DNA" at the American Music Awards later that year, becoming the first K-pop group to perform at a major US award show. And from there, the ARMY continued to grow even larger.

BTS was unstoppable. Shortly after the release of *Map of the Soul: Persona*, which included notable tracks like "Boy with Luv" featuring Halsey, and "Mikrokosmos," a song dedicated to their fans, BTS embarked on their first-ever worldwide stadium tour in the summer of 2018. After wrapping up their incredible tour, the group hit the stage at the 2020 Grammys as the first Korean act to perform at the award show. Without losing momentum, the boys kept breaking records with *Map of the Soul: 7*, the bestselling album in Korea of all time. Then they released their first song entirely recorded in English, "Dynamite." The choice to record an all-English song came as a surprise to the boys as well as the fans. Though they hadn't planned for it, once BTS members listened to the demo, they loved the song and decided to take on the challenge and show a different side to their fans. Later that year, the band made history once again when "Dynamite" was nominated for a Grammy. The Bangtan Boys continued to release English-language singles in 2021, starting with "Butter," then "Permission to Dance."

BTS's musical achievements know no bounds—from snagging Grammy nominations to becoming the bestselling artist in Korean history, there's barely an award or record the group hasn't achieved. But beyond their talents on and off stage, it's the lasting impact they have on ARMY that truly makes them special and maintains their star status. Since ARMY—Adorable Representative MC for Youth—was established, the boys have genuinely connected with their fans and even spoken about being inspired by ARMY themselves. While focusing on their music and performances, BTS have also led generous philanthropy efforts and advocated for social causes. BTS's "Love Myself" campaign with UNICEF has raised over $3 million to help end violence, bullying, and abuse among children and young people. ARMY has matched BTS's large-scale donations to organizations like Black Lives Matter and has also made its own charitable gestures. For J-Hope's birthday in 2019, ARMY in Korea donated 128 sacks of rice to the member's hometown of Gwangju in his honor.

Just days after releasing *Proof*, a special anthology album curated for fans, in June 2022, BTS announced they would be going on a hiatus to work on solo opportunities and fulfill other responsibilities outside of the group. Since then, several members have launched individual projects, like J-Hope's first solo album *Jack in the Box* and Jungkook's collaboration with Charlie Puth, "Left and Right." But we're grateful the boys have continued to stay active on *Run BTS*, social media, public engagements, and more. They held a free, electrifying in-person concert in Busan, Korea and even starred in a revealing docuseries that followed their journey to stardom over the past decade. Whether our boys are together as BTS or as talented solo acts, ARMY will continue to support them and show up for their biases and the rest of the group!

PART

" *Dynamite* "

Welcome to your personal space to muse about your favorite group! Each chapter, named after an unforgettable and catchy song, will explore a different aspect of BTS, helping you reflect on the qualities that make the group extraordinary and to think up epic scenarios. Whether it's discussing their significant impact on the world or imagining hanging out with the crew, you'll enjoy jumping into it all! These chapters also test your BTS knowledge with trivia questions along the way. Get creative and make this journal your own. Now prepare to channel the energy of "Dynamite" and light up the pages ahead.

ONE

CHAPTER ONE

"DNA"

THEIR BUTTERY VOCALS or outstanding visuals may have caught our attention at first, but BTS's endearing and adorable personalities are ultimately what made us the fans we are today. Through their interviews, V Lives, cooking series, and more, we've learned much about their quirky yet lovable "DNA." One of their most popular songs, the track marked a new chapter for their career back in 2017. In these next few pages, put yourself in each BTS member's shoes. From picturing what kind of friend each boy might be to looking back on the band's most revealing moments, you'll find yourself diving deep into BTS's identity in this chapter.

The members are known to be super-loyal to each other and their fans. If you could confide in one of the boys, which member would you trust the most with your biggest secret? Why would you count on him the most?

> _____
> **BTS MEMBER**

If you were struggling with school, fighting with your parents, or going through another hardship in your life, which member of BTS would you go to for advice and a shoulder to lean on? What makes you think he would give the best advice? How would he help you cope?

> _____
> **BTS MEMBER**

While any of the boys would obviously be welcome in your inner circle, which BTS member do you think would fit into your friend group the best? What role do you think he would have in your crew?

BTS MEMBER

You're in a group text with all the members of BTS. Who do you think would blow up your phone? Only send voice notes and never texts? Send the most TikToks? Simply lurk and forget to answer?

?

Recorded in both Korean and Japanese, "DNA" is one of the band's lead tracks. Which album did the song first appear on?

(A) *Map of the Soul: 7*

(B) *Face Yourself*

(C) *Love Yourself: Answer*

(D) *Love Yourself: Her*

My Answer

ANSWER C. First released in September 2017, "DNA" is the lead single from BTS's fifth extended-play album.

You find yourself in an alternate universe. In this awesome reality, you're one of the Bangtan Boys. Who would you want to be? How would you spend your day? What parts of his life would you lean into? Is he known for any favorite hobbies you would want to try?

BTS MEMBER

How would you describe each BTS member's personality in one word? Think about their defining personality traits. Explain your reasoning for each quality.

RM

JUNGKOOK

V

JIMIN

J-HOPE

SUGA

JIN

ARMY is constantly replaying, rereading, and sharing BTS's many exciting, funny, or crush-worthy interviews via video and in articles, many of which reveal the boys' personalities. Rank your top five favorite interviews the group has done.

1 _____

2 _____

3 _____

4 _____

5

Each member is surely endearing in his own way, but if you could only choose one favorite, who is the most charming BTS member to you? Is your answer the same as your bias?

_____
BTS MEMBER

_____

_____

_____

_____

_____

_____

Though BTS can be described in many ways, what are five traits you would use to describe the group as a whole? Would you call BTS silly, caring, and adventurous, for example? What comes to mind when you think about the band's identity?

ONE

TWO

THREE

FOUR

FIVE

Imagine that two of the boys have been transferred to your class in school! Who would you most like to show around and get to know? Do you think they would be good classmates, or would you want to disrupt the class with them? Describe the kind of experience you imagine with each guy.

1

2

They may not be comedians, but BTS members do have their hilarious moments. Who is the funniest member to you? Whose sense of humor matches yours? Whose jokes make you laugh the most?

_____

_____

_____

_____

_____

_____

_____

_____

Whether you're bingeing episodes of *Run BTS* or watching the band's latest funny interview, there are so many adorably hilarious clips of the group. Rank the top five funniest moments of BTS you've come across.

1 _____

2 _____

3 _____

4 _____

5 _____

?

The first member of BTS joined Big Hit Entertainment in 2010, and the rest followed shortly after to form the incredible group. Who were the first three members to join what would become the Bangtan Boys?

A RM, Suga, J-Hope

B RM, Jungkook, V

C Suga, J-Hope, Jin

D Jimin, RM, J-Hope

My Answer

ANSWER A. The rap line was the first to join because BTS was originally supposed to be a hip-hop group.

Which BTS member feels most like family to you and why? Think about the member you relate to the most, who you can most depend on, and who makes you feel comfortable and most at home.

```
_____
                BTS MEMBER
```

If you could pick one BTS member to have dinner with your family, who would it be? Who do you think would get along best with your guardians or siblings? How do you think he would fit into your family dynamic?

```
_____
                BTS MEMBER
```

You're putting together the superlatives for your school yearbook. What superlative would you give each BTS member? Think of titles like Class Clown, Most Likely to Be President, Best Dressed, Most Likely to Win the Lottery, etc.

RM

_____
_____
_____

JUNGKOOK

_____
_____
_____

V

_____
_____
_____

JIMIN

_____
_____
_____

J-HOPE

_____
_____
_____

SUGA

_____
_____
_____

JIN

_____
_____
_____

Each BTS member has multiple nicknames bestowed on them by both fans and one another. Write down which nickname you believe best represents each member. Why does that name suit him? Who gave him that nickname? Is there a funny story behind it?

RM

_____

_____

_____

JUNGKOOK

_____

_____

_____

V

_____

_____

_____

JIMIN

_____

_____

_____

J-HOPE

_____

_____

_____

SUGA

_____

_____

_____

JIN

_____

_____

_____

The boys' V Lives reveal rare insights into their quirky personalities and day-to-day lives. Rank your top five favorite V Live moments, keeping in mind which clips have made you laugh or taught you something new about the members.

1

2

3

4

5

In many ways, BTS's music has shaped our identities. Choose one BTS song to be associated with your name or identity. What would it be? Why do you identify with this song? Explain your pick.

SONG TITLE

When you initially discovered BTS, what was your first impression of each member? Did you automatically have a bias? Reflect on the early days of your fandom and write about what you thought of each of the boys.

RM

_____
_____
_____

JUNGKOOK

_____
_____
_____

V

_____
_____
_____

JIMIN

_____
_____
_____

J-HOPE

_____
_____
_____

SUGA

_____
_____
_____

JIN

_____
_____
_____

Though BTS is now one of the most successful groups in the world, the boys overcame many obstacles and challenges in their early days. Which member almost left the band before his debut?

A Jungkook **C** Jimin

B J-Hope **D** V

My Answer

ANSWER B. In the documentary Burn the Stage: The Movie, J-Hope revealed that he wanted to quit to pursue a dance career, but Jungkook convinced him to stay.

Within the group, there are special bonds among different members. Which two BTS members do you think bring out the best in one another? What do you love about their friendship?

_____
BTS MEMBERS

_____

_____

_____

_____

_____

_____

_____

BTS members aren't afraid to show their affection and appreciation for each other and for ARMY. Rank your top five sweetest moments from the boys, whether they were interacting with one another, other celebrities, or fans.

1 _____

2 _____

3 _____

4 _____

5 _____

BTS's identity has evolved over the past decade. How do you think the band's identity has changed for the good? What do you feel is different since their debut?

_____

_____

_____

_____

_____

_____

_____

_____

_____

_____

While there are so many K-pop groups out there, there is only *one* BTS. What about BTS's identity makes them stand out from any other boy band or K-pop group? What do you think sets them apart personality-wise?

_____

_____

_____

_____

_____

_____

_____

_____

After nine years together, BTS have made a lot of changes to their sound. From School Trilogy (BTS's first era) to Be, which musical era was your favorite for each BTS member? Consider each boy's talent and personality, as well as the visuals used during each era.

RM

_____

_____

_____

JUNGKOOK

_____

_____

_____

V

_____

_____

_____

JIMIN

_____

_____

_____

J-HOPE

_____

_____

_____

SUGA

_____

_____

_____

JIN

_____

_____

_____

V has talked about feeling torn between V, his identity as a performer, and Kim Tae-hyung, his identity when he is around his inner circle. How do you imagine each member's presence differs from how he acts around friends and family? What aspects of his identity do you think remain the same?

RM
_____
_____
_____

JUNGKOOK
_____
_____
_____

V
_____
_____
_____

JIMIN
_____
_____
_____

J-HOPE
_____
_____
_____

SUGA
_____
_____
_____

JIN
_____
_____
_____

?

Which BTS member is now nicknamed "Car Door Guy" after a viral moment at the 2015 Melon Music Awards?

A Jin   **C** Suga

B Jimin   **D** RM

My Answer

Each BTS member has a unique and equally great personality type! Which member's personality do you think is most like yours? Who do you think you would get along best with? Who do you have the most in common with? Who do you think is your total opposite?

CHAPTER TWO

"MIC DROP"

WHILE WE'RE OBSESSED WITH BTS for too many reasons to count, music is ultimately at the heart of the boy band. In this chapter, you'll reflect on BTS's vast discography, rank some of your favorites, and dive into your relationship with BTS through their music. Named after the band's standout hit with Steve Aoki, "Mic Drop" will get you thinking about BTS's electrifying music videos, meaningful lyrics, and mesmerizing performances! Whether you're picturing yourself singing karaoke with your bias or musing about the one song that can always cheer you up, hit "play" on your BTS playlist to get into the mood.

If you could make a "starter pack" playlist for your friends or family members who are unfamiliar with BTS or are not yet fans, what five songs would you include? Why would you choose these songs?

ONE

TWO

THREE

FOUR

FIVE

Think back to when you initially discovered BTS. What's the first song you heard that made you interested in their music? Where were you when you listened to that song? What caught your attention about the track?

> _____
> SONG TITLE

_____

_____

_____

_____

_____

There are so many reasons you could become ARMY, but when it comes to BTS's music, what's the one song that turned you into a true fan? Why did that song have such an impact?

> _____
> SONG TITLE

_____

_____

_____

_____

_____

_____

Since they formed as a group, BTS have released a variety of full studio, mini, and anthology albums. If you could only listen to one BTS song on each of the following albums for the rest of your life (I know, I know!), which songs would you choose?

- ⦿ *Dark & Wild*

- ⦿ *Wings*

- ⦿ *Face Yourself*

- ⦿ *Love Yourself: Tear*

- ⦿ *Map of the Soul: 7*

- ⦿ *Be*

- ⦿ *Proof*

BTS has released so much awesome music. Which track do you think is the band's most underrated and deserves more hype? Why this song specifically? What aspects of the song deserve more recognition?

SONG TITLE

Our talented members of BTS have dropped a fun mix of studio albums, compilations, and extended plays in Korean, Japanese, and English, spanning many different styles of music. Rank your top five favorite albums.

ONE

TWO

THREE

FOUR

FIVE

?

Among BTS's record-breaking hits, which song (at the time of its release) broke the record for most-streamed track on *Spotify* in the first twenty-four hours of its release?

A "Butter"

B "Dynamite"

C "Boy with Luv"

D "Fake Love"

My Answer

ANSWER A. After "Butter" was released in May 2021, it reached over twenty million streams on Spotify within twenty-four hours.

40

Every BTS song makes fans feel *all* the feels in many different ways. Which track would you listen to for each of the following situations and why?

When you want a good cry:

When you're falling in love:

When you're feeling hopeful:

When you want to break into a dance:

When it's raining outside:

From hip-hop and emo rock to EDM and pop, BTS's music spans different genres and styles, showing how impressive and talented all of the members are. Which style of music is your personal favorite? Why?

BTS have come out with over two hundred songs throughout their successful career, many of which are now chart-topping hits. What are your top five favorite songs of all time from the band?

ONE

TWO

THREE

FOUR

FIVE

What do you think is each BTS member's standout track? What track comes to mind when you think of each of the boys? For each member, choose one song he truly shined in, and explain why you picked each.

RM

_____
_____
_____

JUNGKOOK

_____
_____

V

_____
_____

JIMIN

_____
_____

J-HOPE

_____
_____

SUGA

_____
_____
_____

JIN

_____
_____
_____

BTS have released over *seventy* music videos since their debut in 2013. Talk about ambitious! Which music video is your favorite and why? Is your favorite music video different from your favorite song?

MUSIC VIDEO

The boys have starred in a ton of music videos featuring a range of different types of choreography, visuals, and concepts. Rank your top five favorite music videos.

ONE

TWO

THREE

FOUR

FIVE

?

Many consider BTS's first American award show performance as a breakthrough moment. Which award show marked BTS's US television debut?

- **A** Grammy Awards
- **B** Billboard Music Awards
- **C** MTV Video Music Awards
- **D** American Music Awards

My Answer

ANSWER D. BTS made history at the 2017 AMAs, delivering an electrifying performance of fan-favorite "DNA."

While every member always looks incredible in every music video, you have to admit—you've got some favorites. Which music video stood out the most for each member's appearance? What music video made each boy seem especially adorable, soulful, or really visually attractive to you?

RM

_____
_____
_____

JUNGKOOK

_____
_____
_____

V

_____
_____
_____

JIMIN

_____
_____
_____

J-HOPE

_____
_____
_____

SUGA

_____
_____
_____

JIN

_____
_____
_____

Sadly, not every BTS song comes with a music video. What are three songs that *need* to have a music video? How do you think each of these tracks would benefit from a visual element?

ONE

TWO

THREE

Pitch a music video idea for your favorite B-side. What song would you choose? If you could serve as a director with an unlimited budget, what would your theme/concept be? How would you represent this theme visually? Write about your proposed idea.

BTS has collaborated with iconic musicians like Coldplay, Halsey, Steve Aoki, and Charli XCX. If you could choose the artist for BTS's next collaboration, who would it be? Why did you choose this pairing? Describe what this ultimate collab would be like performing or in a music video.

ARTIST

If BTS were to cover music from any other K-pop group, which group would you pick? How do you think BTS would change the sound to make it different from the original? Describe why you would pick this group.

K-POP GROUP

From concert tours and showcases to live award show gigs, BTS has delivered countless performances that we've replayed constantly! Rank your top five favorite performances from the band.

1

2

3

4

5

From RM and Jin's "Trouble" to V and Jin's "Even If I Die, It's You," members have performed duets with each other. Which two members who have yet to sing a duet together would you like to see collaborate next? What would the vibe of their song be?

_____
BTS MEMBERS

_____

_____

_____

_____

_____

BTS loves a good _noraebang_ sesh. Which BTS song is your go-to karaoke song? Which member would you most like to sing that song with?

_____
SONG TITLE

_____

_____

_____

_____

_____

_____

?

BTS has released more than seventy music videos over the years. Which one has the most views on *YouTube*?

A "DNA"

B "Mic Drop"

C "Dynamite"

D "Boy with Luv"

My Answer

ANSWER D. With over 1.5 billion views, "Boy with Luv" featuring Halsey is the band's most viewed music video to date.

51

While a BTS concert with all seven members would be most ideal, if only one subunit of BTS were to have a concert, which would you most like to see? The rap or vocal line? The *maknae* or *hyung* line? The 3Js or Bermuda triangle? Why did you pick this group?

_____

_____

_____

_____

_____

_____

_____

_____

_____

You're at a BTS concert on their next world tour. If you were called onto the stage to sing one song with them, which one would it be? Why? What would that experience be like?

_____
SONG TITLE

_____

_____

_____

_____

_____

BTS's rap line consists of RM, J-Hope, and Suga, and their vocal line includes Jungkook, Jimin, Jin, and V. If you could choose one member from the rap line to freestyle rap for you, who would it be? Who would you pick to serenade you from the vocal line?

_____

BTS MEMBER

BTS songs are made extra-special by their earnest lyrics. Each song can adapt to a ton of different situations in our daily lives! Which song has your favorite lyrics? Which lines in particular resonate with you the most? How do those lyrics make you feel?

SONG TITLE

BTS doesn't just make amazing melodies—the band's lyrics are often meaningful and comment on larger themes and social topics. Which lyric or line from a BTS song means the most to you? What do you think of when you hear this lyric?

_____

_____

_____

_____

_____

_____

_____

_____

BTS released their first English-language song, "Dynamite," in 2020. If you could pick one of the band's Korean songs to be released in English, which one would you choose? Why?

SONG TITLE

_____

_____

_____

_____

_____

_____

?

BTS released their first full-length studio album, *Dark & Wild*, in August 2014. How many tracks are on this debut album?

A Nine   **C** Fourteen

B Thirteen   **D** Sixteen

My Answer

ANSWER C. The boys recorded the album's lead single, "Danger," in a garage in Los Angeles.

CHAPTER THREE

"PERMISSION TO DANCE"

BTS BRINGS THEIR MUSIC TO LIFE through their epic choreography and brilliant moves that always leave us wanting more. Ahead, you'll muse about the group's cool techniques and styles and imagine various scenarios that'll have you daydreaming about dancing with the boys in real life. Picturing a dance collaboration between BTS and another one of your favorite groups? Reflecting on your most-watched dance breaks and practices? Thinking about which member could teach you his challenging choreography? You'll find it all in "Permission to Dance," a chapter dedicated to the upbeat energy and positivity of BTS's 2021 hit.

While the Bangtan Boys often dance the same choreography and are super in sync, each member has his own amazing flair. In five words or less, describe each BTS member's dance style.

RM:

JUNGKOOK:

V:

JIMIN:

J-HOPE:

SUGA:

JIN:

If you were hosting a freestyle dance battle between two BTS members, who would you pick to compete? What type of music would you play? Who do you think would ultimately win?

J-Hope, Jimin, and Jungkook might make up BTS's dance line, but each member in the group has his own style. Whose dance style do you like the most? What do you like about his moves? What makes his style different from the others?

```
 _____
|                                                  |
|        _____        |
|                  BTS MEMBER                      |
|_____|
```

_____

_____

_____

_____

_____

While BTS's dance line tackles the group's most challenging choreography, every member can hold his own on the dance floor. Outside of the three members in the dance line, who do you think is the best dancer? What do you love about his style?

```
 _____
|                                                  |
|        _____        |
|                  BTS MEMBER                      |
|_____|
```

_____

_____

_____

_____

_____

Whether it's a synchronized group performance or a solo routine from just one of the boys, BTS's choreography is versatile, totally eye-catching, and creative. With both group and individual performances in mind, rank your top five favorite BTS choreographies.

1

2

3

4

5

If you were introducing BTS's choreography to a beginner dancer, what three songs would you recommend they learn first? Why would you suggest them? What dances do you think are the easiest to pick up on?

ONE

TWO

THREE

In the "Permission to Dance" music video, the members and other performers are seen dancing in several settings. Which of these settings did they *not* dance in?

A School hallway

B Desert

C Laundromat

D Restaurant

My Answer

You're throwing a BTS-themed dance party. What ten songs are must-plays for the party? Think about the tracks that will get people excited and heading to the dance floor.

1 _____

2 _____

3 _____

4 _____

5 _____

6 _____

7 _____

8 _____

9 _____

10 _____

From BTS's hip-hop-inspired "No More Dream" choreography to their intricate "I Need U" modern dance, the boys have shown impressive range. Which of their choreographed dances do you think is most unique? Describe the moves and why you think they're so special.

_____

_____

_____

_____

_____

_____

_____

From J-Hope's "Boy Meets Evil" dance to Jimin's "Black Swan" solo, each BTS member has performed various individual moves that have blown us away. What is your favorite solo dance for each member?

RM

JUNGKOOK

V

JIMIN

J-HOPE

SUGA

JIN

Whether it's Jin's viral "Super Tuna" dance or the boys' "Go Go" performance as Snow White and the Seven Dwarfs, the band often get silly with their dancing. What do you think are the five funniest dances BTS has performed?

1

2

3

4

5

If BTS were to collaborate with another K-pop group for a dance performance, which group would you like to see dancing with them? What genre of music would you want choreographed? Are there specific songs you'd want featured? Explain why you think these groups would work well together.

K-POP GROUP

If BTS were to cover any boy band's music video, what song would you like to see them re-create? What dance moves in particular do you want to see the boys take for a spin? What do you think their version would look like?

_____

_____

_____

_____

_____

_____

_____

_____

_____

Whether their moves are fast-paced and skilled or emotive and expressive, BTS can master any choreography out there and captivate their audience—especially ARMY! Rank your top five favorite BTS dance moves.

1 _____

2 _____

3 _____

4 _____

5 _____

It's a bummer that not every BTS song has choreography to go with it. What's one song you wish came with choreographed moves? What dance style do you think would pair well with the track?

_____
SONG TITLE

_____
_____
_____
_____
_____
_____
_____

The group frequently shows glimpses of their dance practices before delivering mesmerizing performances at concerts and on TV shows. Which dance practice is your favorite to watch? What's the most intriguing part of the practice? How is the practice different from the band's live performances of the song?

_____
_____
_____
_____
_____
_____
_____
_____

?

While every Bangtan Boy is now a talented dancer, one member actually studied dance in school prior to becoming a trainee at Big Hit. Which member is it?

A Jimin   C J-Hope

B Jin   D RM

My Answer

ANSWER A. Jimin was a top student at Busan High School of Arts, where he studied contemporary dance.

If you could receive a dance lesson from one BTS member, who would you choose? What kind of teacher do you think he would be? Patient? Understanding? Strict? What awesome move or routine of his would you want to learn and master?

BTS MEMBER

You were lucky enough to score tickets to BTS's next world tour! If you were called onto the stage to participate in dancing to one song, which one would you want it to be? Why? Would you dance freestyle or follow the band's choreography? Describe what the experience would be like.

SONG TITLE

Like many K-pop groups, the Bangtan Boys often implement dance breaks—breaks in songs dedicated to showing off their dance moves—in both live performances and music videos. Rank your top five favorite dance breaks of all time.

1

2

3

4

5

If you could adopt the dance style and skills of one BTS member, who would it be? Do you think this member is the best dancer, or do you just love his vibe? What moves specifically would you want to master yourself?

BTS MEMBER

If you could bring just one member of BTS to your upcoming school dance, who would you choose? Who would hype you up on the dance floor? Who would you and your friends have the most fun with? Explain why you would pick this member.

BTS MEMBER

?

BTS often recruit famous and super-talented choreographers to help design their performances. Which of these choreographers has the group *not* worked with?

A Quick Style

B Mihawk Back

C Rie Hata

D Sienna Lalau

My Answer

BTS has delivered *thousands* of performances over the years, and while some focus more on visuals or vocals, others are all about the choreography. Rank your top five favorite BTS dance performances of all time.

1

2

3

4

5

BTS's dance performances are often very emotive and emotionally powerful. What dance performance in particular brings out all the emotions? What feelings come to mind? What does the performance make you think about?

Many BTS hits, whether old or new, have inspired viral dance challenges on social media. Which popular dance challenges have you tried out for yourself? What's your favorite challenge that BTS has taken part in on TikTok? Why?

New dance challenges of all genres and styles are constantly being introduced all over social media. There's always a new trend! If you directed BTS's next TikTok, what viral dance would you like to see the boys try? Why? How would you instruct them to put their own twist on it?

_____

_____

_____

_____

_____

_____

_____

Some of BTS's choreography is popular all over the Internet, while other pieces aren't as easily recognizable. Which song's choreography do you think deserves more attention from fans? What dance moves and moments in particular are underrated? Why do you think these are not as popular?

_____

_____

_____

_____

_____

_____

All BTS music videos manage to showcase fresh and creative choreography, but not every production may be your style. If you had the opportunity to change the choreography in one music video, which would it be? What would you want to change about it? What style would you prefer instead?

MUSIC VIDEO

The boys have certainly mastered their skills and techniques when it comes to hip-hop dancing. What are five types of dance styles you would like to see BTS explore in their future music videos and performances? Why?

1

2

3

4

5

?

While to an audience, BTS's choreography always appears smooth and synchronized, members have previously opened up about challenging moves. Which song's choreography did BTS reveal to be the most challenging?

A "Dope"
B "Dionysus"
C "Blood Sweat & Tears"
D "ON"

My Answer
_____

ANSWER D. In an interview, most of the members agreed that the exact and technical choreography of "ON" was the hardest.

CHAPTER FOUR

"BOYZ WITH FUN"

THE BANGTAN BOYS KNOW HOW TO HAVE FUN, and in this chapter, you'll join in on their adventures through imaginative prompts about traveling, eating, and shopping, to name a few. Picture what it would be like to spend time with BTS at their go-to spots in Seoul, share your favorite hobbies with your bias, and borrow pieces from the most stylish member's closet. In "Boyz with Fun," titled after the energizing 2015 track, you'll explore all of that and more. Get ready to dream up scenarios about hanging with the boys as you navigate through this chapter.

Although all the boys are friends, some members share a closer bond than others. From Vkook to Sope, there are endless ships within the group. Which BFF pairing is your personal favorite? What have they done together that you've loved? What would you do if the three of you could hang out?

BTS MEMBERS

If you could hang out with your bias for just one day, where would you go? What would you do with him? What questions would you want to ask? Write out every detail of this perfect day.

BTS members are quite private about their personal lives, but they still include their families in events. They often invite their parents and siblings to concerts and give family members sweet shout-outs. If you could hang out with one member and his family for the day, who would you choose?

BTS MEMBER

Members of BTS love their pets and often share photos of their adorable furry family members. If you could hang out with a member and one of his pets, which one would it be? Maybe draw yourself playing with the BTS member and his pet or write a poem about them!

You can hang out with each member of BTS at just one location for a day. Whether it's a petting zoo, cool clothing store, or yummy restaurant, where would you take each one, keeping in mind each member's interests?

RM	
JUNGKOOK	
V	
JIMIN	
J-HOPE	
SUGA	
JIN	

BTS's cooking show *BTS Recipe* has given fans a fun look at the members whipping up tasty dishes in the kitchen. Which member would you want to cook your favorite meal with? What would you want to talk about over dinner with him?

The boys have been spotted hanging out at various restaurants, stores, and public spaces around Seoul. If you could spend the day with BTS in their city, what five cool spots would you like to hit? Based on your interests and theirs, think of what places are must-sees in Seoul.

1

2

3

4

5

BTS's go-to restaurant pre-debut, *Yoojung Sikdang*, and the famous BT21 store and café are some of the many iconic locations ARMY must visit when they travel to Korea. As a BTS fan, what are the top five places on your bucket list if you visit Korea?

1

2

3

4

5

?

The members of BTS love to cook and eat together. There's one member who is known to be the biggest foodie, however. Who is it?

A Jungkook **C** Jimin

B RM **D** Jin

My Answer

BTS pay a visit to your hometown for a day. What places would you show them around your neighborhood? Where would you take them to eat, get coffee, and shop? What's a spot that's unique to your town that you would want to introduce them to?

You can take one of the Bangtan Boys to one of your favorite restaurants. What restaurant would you bring this member to? What cuisine is it? Why do you think he would appreciate this place? What would you recommend ordering for the table?

Aside from music and dance, each well-rounded member of BTS has various hobbies outside of his career, whether it's RM's biking or V's painting. Rank your top five favorite hobbies of the members.

ONE

TWO

THREE

FOUR

FIVE

While it's hard to picture the boys studying, taking tests, and participating in school activities, imagine bringing one of them with you to school for the day. What do you think his favorite class would be? His least favorite? Why?

Imagine that you can travel anywhere in the world with the boys of BTS. Where would you want to go and why? What are your must-dos for this city/country? What activities would you want to do with the boys? What sights would you explore?

As we have seen on *Run BTS*, the boys are into entertaining, dynamic activities like mafia games, water sports, treasure hunts, and more. If you could join one of their games, what would you choose? Why would you want to be a part of this activity?

From the group's first-ever show, *BTS Rookie King: Channel Bangtan*, to the beloved *Run BTS*, the boys have starred in many of their own fun and intimate variety shows, giving fans an inside look at their personalities and lives. Rank your top five favorite BTS variety shows.

1

2

3

4

5

We know BTS enjoy trying new games and activities. What's one hobby of yours that you would like to introduce the members to? Imagine teaching and telling them all about it. Describe what it would be like to spend time together doing this activity with them.

From playing quiz shows to fighting off zombies at an amusement park, *Run BTS* shows the members taking on exciting challenges and games. When did the fan-favorite variety show first air?

A 2014   **C** 2016

B 2015   **D** 2017

My Answer

From "BTS Heardle" to "BTS World," there are countless fan video games out there for ARMY to enjoy. Of the ones you've played, which one is your favorite? Which game makes you feel most connected to BTS?

_____

_____

_____

_____

_____

_____

_____

_____

The _Run BTS_ series has allowed ARMY to feel close to BTS as we've learned more about their personalities and what it would be like to hang out with them. Rank your top five favorite _Run BTS_ episodes.

ONE _____

TWO _____

THREE _____

FOUR _____

FIVE _____

We've seen the boys play and have fun with different sports. If you could play one sport with the group as a whole, which one would you pick? What position would you want to play? Which members do you think would get competitive?

You're going to an amusement park for the day with BTS. What park would you go to? What rides would you get on? Who do you think would join you for the thrilling roller coasters? What food would you get? Describe your dream day at the park with the boys.

You're organizing a movie marathon with the members of BTS. Based on the boys' and your favorite films, what five movies would you include in the lineup? Would you have a theme? What snacks would you provide?

1 _____

2 _____

3 _____

4 _____

5 _____

_____

_____

_____

_____

Similarly, if you were to plan a TV marathon with the boys, what five television series would you plan to watch? What shows would you like to binge together and discuss while watching?

ONE _____

TWO _____

THREE _____

FOUR _____

FIVE _____

?

The BTS members are animal lovers and have owned dogs, cats, and even sugar gliders. Which member's pet lived with the boys at one point?

A J-Hope   **C** Jungkook

B Suga   **D** V

My Answer

ANSWER   D. V's dog Yeontan, a Pomeranian nicknamed Tannie, became a part of the BTS family when he lived in the dorm with the boys.

Each member of the Bangtan Boys has a unique sense of style. If you could choose one member to take you shopping in Seoul, who would it be? Why would you choose him? What would you buy? Draw your K-pop-inspired outfits.

The boys are all super-fashionable in different ways. If you could steal pieces from just one member's closet, who would you choose? What pulls you toward his style? Which outfits in particular have stood out to you?

> BTS MEMBER

_____

_____

_____

_____

_____

Whether they're wearing colorful satin suits at the 2020 American Music Awards or sleek identical tuxedos at the 2019 Grammys, BTS has *slayed* some iconic coordinated fashion moments for red carpets, music videos, performances, and more. Rank your top five favorite looks from BTS as a group.

1 _____

2 _____

3 _____

4 _____

5 _____

BTS Recipe has shown us the boys' recipes for delicious Korean foods like Jin's *janchi guksu*, Jungkook's sweet potato *mattang*, and RM's *japchae*. From the dishes they've shared, what five recipes would you want to re-create the most?

ONE _____

TWO _____

THREE _____

FOUR _____

FIVE _____

The group has released tons of official merchandise over the years. What are some of your favorite BTS merch items that you own? What's something you wish they would sell in the future?

_____

_____

_____

_____

_____

_____

_____

_____

?

BTS members are always super-supportive of one another, exchanging sweet gestures and thoughtful presents. Which member gifted Suga a coffee truck to support him?

A Jin   **C** J-Hope

B V   **D** RM

My Answer
_____

ANSWER C. J-Hope sent Suga a coffee truck while Suga was filming the "Daechwita" music video. Sope is such a cute ship!

CHAPTER FIVE

"BOY WITH LUV"

IF YOU'RE A FAN OF THE BANGTAN BOYS, you *definitely* have a bias. Whether you admire this member's talents, find him wildly attractive, or swoon over his personality, you've got your reasons. You can get into all things romance and more in "Boy with Luv," based on BTS's ultra-popular collab with Halsey. In this chapter, you'll dive into your obsession with your bias (and bias wrecker!) and imagine what the members are like as boyfriends or where they'd take someone on a first date. Turn on your go-to romantic playlist from the boys and get ready to daydream about your crush.

The first question every ARMY gets asked is likely this one: Who is your ultimate BTS bias? Why is this member your favorite? What do you think your bias says about you?

```
                    BTS MEMBER
```

_____

_____

_____

_____

_____

_____

Reflect on the first time you realized you were in love with your bias. Describe the moment you knew your bias was *your bias* and was the one you'd spend time daydreaming about. How did you feel? What about him were you drawn to?

_____

_____

_____

_____

_____

_____

_____

Fans also go through different phases of their fandom. Is your initial bias, from when you first became ARMY, still your bias today? If so, what about him has made you stay devoted? If not, why did your bias change?

From the silly Suga to the adorably shy Jungkook, all the Bangtan Boys are beyond lovable, whether they're your bias or not. Name one trait you love the most about each member.

RM	
JUNGKOOK	
V	
JIMIN	
J-HOPE	
SUGA	
JIN	

While all fans have their opinions about their biases, we forget that BTS members themselves might have their own as well. Just for fun, if each boy had to pick, who do you think his BTS bias would be? Explain your reasoning for each member.

RM

JUNGKOOK

V

JIMIN

J-HOPE

SUGA

JIN

With an amazing group like BTS, it can be unthinkable to pick just *one* bias. Who is your bias wrecker? Which member has made you rethink or question your bias? What made you waver?

```
BTS MEMBER
```

Your ultimate bias is important, but your ultimate bias wrecker can definitely catch your attention too. If you could be BFFs with either your bias or bias wrecker, who would you choose? Why do you think this member would make for a better best friend?

Your bias is obviously perfect in every form. But if you had to pick, what's your absolute favorite look that your bias has rocked? Is it a specific outfit, hair color, hairstyle, or makeup? Draw your favorite look in the space provided.

There are many words and phrases that BTS and their fans now use as part of their daily vocabulary. What does "I purple you" mean to ARMY?

A "I admire you."

B "I love you."

C "I respect you."

D "I see you."

My Answer
_____

Your BTS bias is probably chosen for a combination of his looks, vibe, personality, and musical ability. Considering just his talents as an artist, rank the top five songs you think your bias shines in.

ONE

TWO

THREE

FOUR

FIVE

Every ARMY picked their bias for a reason, and sometimes there's overlap with your friends or fellow fans. Do you share the same bias with any of your friends or BTS fans around you? What qualities and moments do you bond over?

You're creating a music playlist dedicated to your bias. What ten songs would you curate? Imagining the member listening to your picks, choose the tracks you would include based on his favorite artists, genres, and sounds.

1
2
3
4
5
6
7
8
9
10

Music videos are an easy way for fans to swoon over their favorite members. Which of the group's music videos does your bias stand out in? Rank the top five music videos you watch for your bias.

ONE

TWO

THREE

FOUR

FIVE

?

BTS members have spoken about their Hollywood crushes in the past. Which member revealed Scarlett Johansson to be his ultimate celebrity crush?

A Suga

C RM

B Jin

D Jimin

My Answer

ANSWER   A. In the same interview, V and Jimin both chose Rachel McAdams as their celebrity crush.

110

BTS is divided between the *hyung* line, with RM, Jin, Suga, and J-Hope, and the *maknae* line, with Jimin, V, and Jungkook. Which line are you more biased toward? Why do you gravitate toward this line?

From live performances and award shows to V Lives and variety shows, there's so much content in which you can thirst over your bias. Rank your top five favorite BTS moments featuring your bias.

1

2

3

4

5

BTS members are *extremely* private about their dating lives. Though we don't know much about each one's romantic history, based on individual hobbies and interests, where do you think each member would take someone on a first date? Write out how you think each date would go.

RM

JUNGKOOK

V

JIMIN

J-HOPE

SUGA

JIN

Based on the few details the group has shared about romantic interests, what do you think is each member's type? List personality traits and hobbies that you think each boy might value and look for.

RM
_____
_____
_____

JUNGKOOK
_____
_____
_____

V
_____
_____
_____

JIMIN
_____
_____
_____

J-HOPE
_____
_____
_____

SUGA
_____
_____
_____

JIN
_____
_____
_____

All the BTS members might make you swoon, but who do you think is the most romantic of the seven? Who can you picture taking his significant other on fun dates and fairytale adventures?

BTS MEMBER

Imagine a world where the Bangtan Boys share their relationships with their fans and the public. What do you think each member would be like in a relationship? What type of boyfriend do you think each would be?

RM:

JUNGKOOK:

V:

JIMIN:

J-HOPE:

SUGA:

JIN:

While we don't know what kind of boyfriend each member might be, based on your predictions, who do you think would make the best boyfriend for *you*? Is it your bias? What makes someone the "best" boyfriend? What qualities do you look for, and how does this member fulfill them?

```
_____
                BTS MEMBER
```

?

The BTS boys know how to get romantic in their songs. Which of the following songs includes a dreamy lyric that refers to their love interest as a masterpiece?

A "Miss Right"

B "Just One Day"

C "Serendipity"

D "For You"

My Answer

You're stressed about how to tell your real-life crush you like them, or you are struggling in your relationship. Which member of BTS would you go to for relationship advice and any guidance on your love life? Why do you think he'd give the best advice?

> _____
> BTS MEMBER

_____

_____

_____

_____

_____

A genuine compliment can truly make someone's day. You have the opportunity to give each member of BTS some praise. What would you say to the boys? Write a one-sentence compliment for every member of the group.

RM:
_____
JUNGKOOK:
_____
V:
_____
JIMIN:
_____
J-HOPE:
_____
SUGA:
_____
JIN:

BTS's discography covers a wide range of topics, from politics and mental health to, yes, true love and romance. Rank your top five favorite romantic BTS songs that always manage to pull at your heartstrings.

ONE

TWO

THREE

FOUR

FIVE

BTS have delivered many inspirational, meaningful words to their fans. What is the biggest message BTS has taught you about love, whether romantic or not? Was it a lyric or specific quote from one of the members? Explain how this message impacted you.

BTS fans know how beautiful and significant the band's lyrics can be. What are your favorite BTS lyrics about love? Which lines do you think about when you have a crush, feel butterflies for someone, or want to look for love? List your top five favorites.

1

2

3

4

5

Imagine planning a dream date night with a member of BTS. Who would you want to invite? What would you plan for the two of you? Describe your ideal date with this boy and why you chose him.

BTS MEMBER

Picture organizing a movie night with the Bangtan Boys. What's one rom-com or romantic film you'd pick to watch with the members? Why did you choose this one? Do you think everyone will enjoy this movie? Who would like it the most?

⎨ _____ ⎬
FILM TITLE

_____

_____

_____

_____

_____

Each BTS member is *obviously* attractive in his own way, but some people are attracted to certain members over others. Which member caught your eye first, from looks/style alone? Why did he catch your attention? Is this member also your bias?

⎨ _____ ⎬
BTS MEMBER

_____

_____

_____

_____

_____

?

"If you want to love others, I think you should love yourself first" is a quote BTS fans often lean on during difficult times. Which member said this inspiring line?

A V

C Jin

B Suga

D RM

My Answer

ANSWER D. In an interview, RM spoke about how the most important love is self-love.

CHAPTER SIX

"LIFE GOES ON"

BTS IMPACTS EVERY FAN DIFFERENTLY. BTS has gotten you through hardships in your life or empowered you to take a big step. Their impact is also global—the Bangtan Boys have forever changed the world with their lasting legacy and influence on K-pop and music and their ongoing commitment to philanthropy. Titled "Life Goes On," this chapter explores that impact, diving into how the group has influenced our lives in many ways. You'll write a letter to the boys about what they mean to you and think back on all the times their uplifting music has helped you become your best self. Get ready to show your deep appreciation for BTS!

From their music to their advocacy, the boys have inspired and motivated fans in so many different ways. What is the most important thing that BTS has taught you? What other life lessons have the boys taught you? What lesson will you remember forever?

Consuming BTS all day, every day has definitely influenced fans' lives. How has BTS shaped your life? What aspects of your personality and identity have been shaped by them? In what ways do you think they have changed you?

_____

_____

_____

_____

_____

_____

_____

_____

Being a member of ARMY is a part of who you are. In your opinion, how does being ARMY affect your daily life and values? How do you think ARMY makes you a better person?

_____

_____

_____

_____

_____

_____

_____

_____

_____

What are five important things you learned from being ARMY (whether about yourself or others)? How did you come to learn these things? How have these discoveries changed you?

1

2

3

4

5

Of BTS's vast discography, countless songs have been meaningful for fans and casual listeners alike. Whether inspirational or moving, rank the top five most personally influential tracks BTS has released.

ONE

TWO

THREE

FOUR

FIVE

When a BTS fan hears one of the Bangtan Boys' songs in public, it never goes unnoticed. Think back—what's the most unexpected place you've heard a BTS song? What song was it? Why was it such a surprise?

BTS often bring positive vibes and optimistic energy through their music, vlogs, social media, and more. How have BTS helped you get through hard times in your life? Reflect on a specific hardship or obstacle that you overcame with the help of BTS.

Many ARMY members have talked about how BTS encouraged them to make a significant move in their life. What big step did BTS help you take? Was it a song or message from the band? Write about that moment.

Your family and friends have likely seen the positive ways BTS have influenced your life. What do you think your loved ones might say about how the group has inspired and changed you for the better?

?

After it was released in November 2020, "Life Goes On" quickly became a smash hit for its optimistic, hopeful message. Which three members cowrote the track?

A RM, Jungkook, Jimin

B RM, J-Hope, Suga

C Jin, Jimin, Jungkook

D J-Hope, V, Suga

My Answer

ANSWER B. While the trio cowrote the lyrics for the transformative song, Jungkook directed the music video.

130

While every member of BTS is influential in his own way, which member is personally most inspiring to you? Who do you see as a role model? What about this member do you find so admirable? Write about the qualities you're motivated by in this boy.

_____

BTS MEMBER

You have the chance to write a letter to BTS that's guaranteed to be read by the boys. Is there something special you want to tell a specific member? Write your letter here, explaining what the group (and ARMY) means to you.

You can send one special present to the boys. What would you send them? Why would you want to gift the boys this item?

_____

_____

_____

_____

_____

_____

_____

_____

_____

_____

_____

As a BTS fan, many of the group's biggest moments have become some of your own. Rank the top five BTS moments that are most memorable to you.

1 _____

2 _____

3 _____

4 _____

5 _____

Over the years, fans have been following BTS's journey as closely as they can. What's one particular story or moment about BTS that touched your heart? Why did this story have such a lasting impact on you? Describe the moment.

If a friend or family member were looking for encouragement and inspiration, which BTS track would you recommend? How do you think this song would comfort them? What would you hope they got out of listening to it?

SONG TITLE

BTS's music can mean different things to every fan. Some albums make you think about optimism and fun, while others allow you to reflect on yourself and the people around you. Rank the top five most impactful BTS albums to you and your life.

ONE

TWO

THREE

FOUR

FIVE

?

The band has so many lyrics that fans love and find super-moving. Which of these inspiring songs encourage listeners to stop running and take a break?

A "Magic Shop"

B "Lost"

C "No More Dream"

D "Paradise"

My Answer

Each era of BTS exudes different energy and vibes, depending on the album and time frame. Which BTS era has influenced you the most? How so? What about this era specifically was most impactful for you?

From thoughtful song lyrics to touching sound bites from videos and interviews, the members of BTS have shared a lifetime's worth of powerful quotes with their fans. Rank the top five quotes from the group that have inspired you the most.

1

2

3

4

5

BTS's words of wisdom and supporting vibes have definitely gotten fans through tough times. If your ARMY friend were struggling through a rough patch, what advice or encouraging words from BTS would you offer them? What quotes or songs do you think could help?

One of the many reasons BTS is beloved is because of the group's generosity and devotion to philanthropic efforts! Which of their charitable moments meant the most to you? Why did this effort in particular move you?

_____

_____

_____

_____

_____

_____

_____

_____

Only a decade into their career, BTS has already produced so many iconic hits. Looking into the future, what are five songs you believe will become true classics? What tracks do you think future fans will know and love?

ONE

TWO

THREE

FOUR

FIVE

?

From inspirational campaigns to large donations, BTS have been recognized for their philanthropic efforts on numerous occasions. Which Bangtan Boy became a member of UNICEF's Honors Club for donating over one hundred million Korean *won* to the organization?

A Jimin **C** Jin

B RM **D** Jungkook

My Answer

ANSWER C. Jin had been quietly donating to the charity organization for months.

Fans love learning about the members' unique interests and hobbies. Beyond albums and licensed BTS merchandise, has the group influenced you to buy any products or try out an experience? Any snacks, books, or fashion items? What made you want to try, or buy, something new?

Picture reading about BTS in history books decades from now. What do you want to be reading about the Bangtan Boys then? What do you hope for their legacy to be? If BTS was remembered for one significant moment or achievement, what would you want it to be?

BTS has been given numerous titles like the world's biggest boy band or the most popular band in the universe. According to you, what qualities make the Bangtan Boys the world's best band?

For some fans, BTS was their introduction to the world of K-pop. What are five things you've learned about K-pop and the Korean music industry since you started stanning BTS? Explain how you dove into these topics.

1

2

3

4

5

There's no doubt that the Bangtan Boys have transformed K-pop and the music industry worldwide. From a fan's perspective, in what ways do you think BTS has changed K-pop forever? How do you think the group has paved the way for other musical acts?

_____

_____

_____

_____

_____

_____

_____

_____

_____

Though BTS's effect on the music industry is powerful, the group's influence transcends the entertainment field. What impact do you believe BTS has had on other industries outside of music? Why do you think so?

_____

_____

_____

_____

_____

_____

_____

_____

?

While BTS inspires many, the group is also influenced by boy bands and artists alike. Which of the following musicians has BTS *not* cited as an inspiration?

- **A** One Direction
- **B** Drake
- **C** Big Bang
- **D** A$AP Rocky

My Answer

ANSWER A. BTS have mostly referred to other K-pop groups, R&B singers, and hip-hop rappers as their main influences.

CHAPTER SEVEN

"MIKROKOSMOS"

ARMY WAS FORMED THROUGH LOVE AND PASSION for the Bangtan Boys, and over the years, BTS's epic fandom has created a beautiful community of fun and inspiring supporters. ARMY will always support BTS, and, in turn, the boys show their devotion for their fans through their music and actions. In this chapter, you'll think deeply about the connection between ARMY and BTS and write about what this unique fandom means to you. From the *Map of the Soul: Persona* album, "Mikrokosmos" is a special song dedicated to the BTS fandom and ARMY. Using this emotional track as inspiration, reflect on all the ways that being ARMY has impacted your life in the prompts ahead!

Every ARMY remembers the moment they became a true fan of the boys. Was it a specific catchy song, moving performance, or funny interview you watched? Describe the moment you fell in love with BTS.

Reflect on when you became an official member of ARMY. Write about the moment you knew you weren't just a fan but were truly committed to the global fandom. What felt different about joining ARMY officially?

Reflect on all the friendships you've made through ARMY. How did you meet your ARMY friends? Are they local or far away from you? Have you ever met them in real life? Write about the friends you met through your shared love of BTS.

_____

_____

_____

_____

_____

_____

_____

_____

ARMY friendships can often grow beyond online interactions. Describe what it would be like to meet your ARMY friends IRL. What would you talk about (aside from BTS, of course)? Where would you hang out? How would you spend the day with them?

_____

_____

_____

_____

_____

_____

_____

_____

You meet a baby ARMY on the Internet or in real life. As a veteran fan, how would you welcome them into the fold? What videos, online forums, or social media accounts would you direct them to? What would you want them to learn about BTS and the fandom?

Many BTS fans were first introduced to the group by their friends. Is there anyone in your life that you converted into ARMY? How did you get them into BTS? What convinced them to join ARMY? How did your mutual love for BTS change your friendship?

From the tight-knit community to the deep connection with the boys, there are endless reasons to love being a BTS fan! Rank your top five favorite aspects of being part of ARMY.

ONE

TWO

THREE

FOUR

FIVE

?

BTS show love for their fans in many different ways, one of which is through their music. What was the boys' first official song dedicated to fans?

A "Pied Piper"

B "2! 3!"

C "Magic Shop"

D "Mikrokosmos"

My Answer

We're so happy that BTS has paid tribute to their fans through much of their music! If you could help the boys write their next song dedicated to ARMY, what message would you want to send to fans? Do you have any title suggestions?

_____

_____

_____

_____

_____

_____

_____

_____

Many members of ARMY have become besties or friends in real life, thanks to their shared passion for BTS. Write about one important person you met that comes to mind and their role in your life now.

_____

_____

_____

_____

_____

_____

_____

_____

_____

From "Mikrokosmos" to "Magic Shop," BTS have written several songs especially for their fans and ARMY throughout their career. Rank your top five favorite BTS tracks dedicated to ARMY.

ONE

TWO

THREE

FOUR

FIVE

Can you imagine BTS bringing a fan onstage and singing to them? If BTS were to choose one lucky fan to join them on the stage for one song, which song do you think they should perform? If you were in this position, what track would you like the boys to serenade you with and why?

Imagine that you're at an intimate fan signing for BTS. If you could ask a question to just one member at the signing, who would you pick and what would you ask? Why is this member-specific question so important to you?

You're lucky enough to have won a private concert session with BTS! At the end of the performance, the group have a Q&A session, and they're open to answering any and all questions from fans. What are five questions you would ask the group?

1

2

3

4

5

You have the opportunity to design official fan merch for BTS! What type of item would you design? Think about what art, photos, and other merchandise you'd like to own, and draw a prototype (or prototypes for different merch) here.

ARMY, the official name of BTS's fandom, was established shortly after the band's debut. What was the exact date?

- **A** June 15, 2013
- **B** June 29, 2013
- **C** July 1, 2013
- **D** July 9, 2013

My Answer

Each fan's experience is unique based on when they first became ARMY! Looking back on when you first discovered the Bangtan Boys, what advice would you give your baby ARMY self? What would you want to tell yourself? What guidance or wisdom would you want to share?

Think back to your early ARMY days. What BTS era ARMY do you consider yourself and why? Whether it was their visuals or music, what got you into BTS during this era?

BTS's ARMY has created major waves not only in the music world and for BTS campaigns but also when it comes to necessary activism and impactful philanthropic efforts. What's one ARMY moment that you were a part of and proud of? Describe the experience and impact that followed.

BTS give back in so many ways. The boys have made charitable donations and launched various campaigns for their fans. What do you think is the sweetest thing BTS has done for a fan? Why does this moment stand out in your memory?

_____

_____

_____

_____

_____

_____

_____

_____

_____

Whether it was one of BTS's fan-dedicated songs, the heartfelt messages to ARMY on live TV, or their many acts of kindness and charity, the band have certainly made fans proud on countless occasions. Rank the top five moments that have made you most proud to be a BTS fan.

1 _____

2 _____

3 _____

4 _____

5 _____

"Worldwide Handsome," "I purple you," and "*Namjooning*" are just some of the few inside jokes and nicknames that only BTS and their biggest fans understand. What are your five favorite BTS words or phrases that would be listed in an ARMY encyclopedia? Why do you love these specific ones?

1

2

3

4

5

ARMY stands for "Adorable Representative MC for Youth." What was BTS originally going to name their fandom before they landed on ARMY?

A K-Diamonds

B I-Lovelies

C Bell

D Carat

My Answer

ANSWER C. The group initially thought of bang wool, which is the Korean word for "bell."

Most ARMY would agree that there's a huge difference between appreciating BTS's music or looks and being a loyal follower. What are five facts about the Bangtan Boys you think only a true fan would know? Write them down here.

1

2

3

4

5

As an expert yourself, what do you think makes a *real* BTS fan? What would you expect other fans to know or care about? What specific catchphrases or quotes should they understand and use? How can you know someone is a true ARMY?

_____

_____

_____

_____

_____

_____

_____

_____

_____

ARMY is one of *many* fandoms in both the K-pop and boy band worlds. In your opinion, what makes ARMY unique compared to the others? If you currently are or have been a part of other fandoms, how is your experience as a BTS fan similar or different?

_____

_____

_____

_____

_____

_____

_____

_____

_____

From an ARMY perspective, what BTS content do you wish existed? Is it reaction videos of the boys watching popular *YouTube* compilations or memes? Is it behind-the-scenes videos from their recording sessions? List five pieces of content you'd like BTS to share in the future and why.

1

2

3

4

5

Through various platforms including social media, live television, and TV shows, BTS have spoken both to and about their fans in beautiful and kind ways. Rank your top five favorite quotes the group has said about ARMY.

1

2

3

4

5

Every ARMY has dreamed about meeting BTS in real life. Describe one fantasy you've had about meeting the boys. Where did you run into them? How did you react? What did you talk about? Write all about the dream scenario.

From *BTS: Burn the Stage* to *Break the Silence: The Movie*, there are multiple documentaries about BTS. If you could create and direct a BTS documentary from a fan's perspective, what parts of their lives would you highlight? What kind of footage would you include?

?

Different members of BTS released solo music just for their fans. Which of the following solo songs was dedicated to ARMY?

A "Outro: Ego" by J-Hope

B "My You" by Jungkook

C "Filter" by Jimin

D "Epiphany" by Jin

My Answer

CHAPTER EIGHT

"YET TO COME"

FANS HAVE ENJOYED THE MEMBERS' ENDEAVORS and projects both as part of BTS and while flying solo. Throughout our years as true ARMY, we've reflected on their beloved discography and highlights over the time they have been together and are excited for what's to come for BTS. Just like the lead single from *Proof* (BTS's anthology album released a few days after the band announced their hiatus in June 2022), in this last chapter, you'll explore those feelings of nostalgia and optimism. Pour your thoughts out on the Bangtan Boys' individual projects, reflect on the most iconic moments of their first chapter, and predict what their future might look like in "Yet to Come."

BTS is known for their collaborations with popular artists, as well as their guest roles in various forms of media. Whether a K-drama appearance, new TV show, or collaboration with a Western musician, what are your dream projects for each member?

RM

JUNGKOOK

V

JIMIN

J-HOPE

SUGA

JIN

From Jungkook's "Left and Right" to J-Hope's *Jack in the Box*, a few of the Bangtan Boys have released solo projects. Whose solo act were/are you most excited for? What projects have you dreamed of the most?

_____

_____

_____

_____

_____

_____

_____

_____

Though some solo projects are still in progress, BTS members have released several individual works. Rank your top five favorite solo projects thus far.

ONE _____

TWO _____

THREE _____

FOUR _____

FIVE _____

Imagine each member of BTS holds a solo concert. Choose one member you would most want to see, and envision what you think his concert would look like. Consider the concept, outfits, sound, set list, and dances while you write about your dream concert!

_____
BTS MEMBER

If each member of BTS were to have a new role in the band, how would you reassign their positions? Who would make a good leader? Who would you want to see as a rapper instead of a vocalist? Who would you want to take on more choreography?

_____

_____

_____

_____

_____

_____

_____

_____

_____

In their solo works, some BTS members have already released brilliant collaborations with other artists. Imagine you could pair individual members with other artists for epic music collabs! Rank your top five dream solo collaborations.

ONE	
TWO	
THREE	
FOUR	
FIVE	

?

The nostalgic "Yet to Come" music video makes references to past music videos throughout the band's career. Which one of the following videos was *not* explicitly referenced?

A "No More Dream"

B "Spring Day"

C "Run"

D "Boy with Luv"

My Answer
_____

We're beyond grateful BTS have become what they are today, but imagine a universe where the boys never made music. If music weren't an option, what career or passion do you think each member would have pursued instead? Based on their interests and skills that you know of, explain your predictions.

RM

_____
_____
_____

JUNGKOOK

_____
_____
_____

V

_____
_____
_____

JIMIN

_____
_____
_____

J-HOPE

_____
_____
_____

SUGA

_____
_____
_____

JIN

_____
_____
_____

What do you predict the next stage of BTS's career will look like? What transformation might the band undergo? How do you think their music and public appearances might change? Rank your top five predictions for the band's future.

ONE _____

TWO _____

THREE _____

FOUR _____

FIVE _____

The emotional "Yet to Come" music video includes a nod to BTS's official debut song, "No More Dream," as they say goodbye to their previous chapters. Looking back on the group's discography since then, what are five songs that best represent BTS over the years?

ONE _____

TWO _____

THREE _____

FOUR _____

FIVE _____

Imagine the Bangtan Boys are going on a "Best of BTS" world tour in the future to perform some of their best songs. What tracks do you hope would make it to the set list? Build your ideal set list for the tour featuring ten BTS songs.

1 _____
2 _____
3 _____
4 _____
5 _____
6 _____
7 _____
8 _____
9 _____
10 _____

The Bangtan Boys have collaborated with huge brands like Louis Vuitton, McDonald's, and Samsung. Which five fashion, food, beauty, or lifestyle companies should BTS work with next? Why would BTS be good partners for these specific brands?

ONE _____

TWO _____

THREE _____

FOUR _____

FIVE _____

If you could plan BTS's next world tour, what would you conceptualize? What outfits, theatrics, and performances would you want to see? What would the stage look like, and the venues in general? What's something unique you could add to the tour? Describe your full vision.

?

In July 2022, J-Hope released *Jack in the Box*, his debut album exploring his personality and vision as a solo artist. How many tracks are on the album?

A Eight

C Ten

B Nine

D Eleven

My Answer

177

From dark and edgy to playful and vibrant, BTS has demonstrated a variety of visual concepts in their music videos, album covers, and performances throughout their career. What types of visuals would you like to see BTS experiment with next? Draw your vision here.

From *Run BTS* to *BTS Recipe*, the boys' variety shows give fans a fun look into their group dynamic. If you could create a show concept about the boys with their new era in mind, what would you pitch? Describe what your dream show about BTS would look like.

You have the chance to cast any of the Bangtan Boys to make a guest appearance on your favorite show! Which member and show would you choose? What role would you want him to play? Would it be a K-drama, a comedy, or something else? Describe your dream cameo.

BTS is truly amazing as is, but imagine you had the opportunity to recruit a member from another K-pop group to BTS. Who would you select? What role would this person fulfill in the band and how do you think they would fit in with BTS's dynamic?

K-POP GROUP MEMBER

BTS have released many well-balanced, popular studio albums throughout their career! If you could select the concept for the group's next studio album, what would your vision be? What genre and music style would you like BTS to tackle next?

While BTS's major releases and performances as a group change, *Run BTS* consistently allows fans to keep up with the boys. They've already taken on a variety of challenges throughout the series. What games and activities would you want to see BTS take on in upcoming seasons?

BTS's reality show *BTS: Bon Voyage* chronicles the group traveling to locations like Hawaii, New Zealand, and Malta, and navigating new environments. If you could choose their next documented destination, where would you pick? Why?

Proof's final disc is dedicated to ARMY, including demo versions of the band's hits, new fan songs, and previously unreleased tracks. Which previously unreleased song made it onto *Proof*?

A "Monterlude"

B "Promise"

C "Still with You"

D "Young Love"

My Answer

RM is a huge fan of the visual arts. He's frequently posted art on *Instagram* and even talked about someday displaying his private collection as an art exhibit! If that aspiration came true, what do you think a museum or gallery curated by RM would look like?

From "Euphoria" to "My You," Jungkook's solo tracks have captured his growth as an artist. What do you hope to see in the *maknae*'s future solo songs, in terms of subject matter, lyrics, melody, and style?

V brought his acting chops to the screen with his debut in *Hwarang: The Poet Warrior Youth*, a K-drama series that aired in 2016. Since then, he's also appeared on variety shows. What type of series and roles would you like to see him playing next?

Jimin's solo album, *PJM1* (aka *Park Jimin 1*), is real, raw, and deeply personal. How do you think his new music is different from what he wrote and sang for the group? In what ways is it the same?

The first of the boys to release a solo album, J-Hope wowed the music scene with *Jack in the Box*. What do you love about the album? What are your favorite tracks? How do you feel about the overall vibe?

Suga may be a gifted rapper, but for his solo music, he's spoken about wanting to continue experimenting with all types of music. What genres and styles would you like to see him exploring in the future?

Resident foodie Jin has talked about how much fun he has appearing on variety shows. If you could create a variety show centered around Jin, what kind of concept would you pitch? Describe your ideal show starring the goofy member.

BTS have already crushed tons of achievements during their career, but there are definitely more to come. And we'll be there rooting for their success! Rank the top five goals you hope the group achieves in the future.

1

2

3

4

5

?

BTS members have shared many dream collaborations over the years, some of which actually happened. Which of the following artists have the boys cited as their dream collaborator?

A Lady Gaga

B Cardi B

C Beyoncé

D Miley Cyrus

My Answer

ANSWER A. At the 2022 Grammys, BTS named Lady Gaga, Olivia Rodrigo, J Balvin, and Snoop Dogg as some of their dream collaborators.

PART

" *Butter* "

Now that you've poured your heart out on some prompts about your all-time favorite boy band, it's time to gather your beloved photos and mementos featuring BTS. Paste your pictures in the following pages and turn your regular journal into a special prized possession dedicated to the Bangtan Boys! Have a photocard of your bias? An album cover? Or a printed-out meme that always makes you laugh? From prints of memorable moments to images you've saved from different magazines, they all belong in "Butter." Get creative and have fun filling the pages ahead, channeling the energy of the epic dance-pop track.

TWO

BIBLIOGRAPHY

Associated Press. "K-Pop Supergroup BTS Says It's Making Time for Solo Projects." June 14, 2022. https://apnews.com/article/ entertainment-music-35fbd8a289cbeefcc553e0711f158cb8.

Benjamin, Jeff. "BTS Explain Concepts Behind 'Love Yourself: Her' Album: 'This Is the Beginning of Our Chapter Two.'" *Billboard*, September 20, 2017. www.billboard.com/music/music-news/bts-love-yourself-her-album-rap-monster-interview-analysis-meaning-7966098/.

Benjamin, Jeff. "BTS' 'Wings' Sets New U.S. Record for Highest-Charting, Best-Selling K-Pop Album." *Billboard*, October 17, 2016. www.billboard.com/pro/ bts-wings-highest-charting-best-selling-kpop-album-billboard-200/.

Bruner, Raisa. "The Mastermind Behind BTS Opens Up about Making a K-Pop Juggernaut." *Time*, October 8, 2019. https://time.com/5681494/ bts-bang-si-hyuk-interview/.

Bruner, Raisa. "Rap Monster of Breakout K-Pop Band BTS on Fans, Fame and Viral Popularity." *Time*, June 28, 2017. https://time.com/4833807/ rap-monster-bts-interview/.

BTS. "Permission to Dance." Directed by Yong Seok Choi and Woogie Kim. July 9, 2021. Music video, 4:59. https://youtu.be/CuklIb9d3fI.

BTS and Halsey. "Boy with Luv." Directed by Yong Seok Choi. April 12, 2019. Music video, 4:12. https://youtu.be/XsX3ATc3FbA.

CNN-News18. "Smooth Like Butter? BTS Shares What They Think Their Hardest Dance Choreography Is." June 3, 2021. www.news18.com/news/ buzz/smooth-like-butter-bts-share-what-they-think-their-hardest-dance-choreography-is-3804902.html.

J.K. "BTS's Fan Song '2! 3!' Tops *Billboard*'s World Digital Song Sales Chart." *Soompi*, November 20, 2018. www.soompi.com/article/1266473wpp/ btss-fan-song-2-3-tops-billboards-world-digital-song-sales-chart.

Kelley, Caitlin. "American Music Awards: K-Pop Superstars BTS to Perform for First Time on U.S. Show." *Hollywood Reporter*, November 3, 2017. www.hollywoodreporter.com/news/music-news/american-music-awards-k-pop-superstars-bts-perform-first-time-american-awards-show-1054714/.

Kim, Grace, and Arin Kim. "BTS Unfiltered: J-Hope Confesses He Tried to Quit BTS." *JoongAng*, April 5, 2018. www.joongang.co.kr/ article/22510996.

Lang, Cady. "Your Guide to the Best BTS Memes on the Internet." *Time*, March 4, 2020. https://time.com/5790598/best-bts-memes.

Lipshutz, Jason. "BTS Thanks Fans for Top Social Artist Win at Billboard Music Awards 2017: Watch." *Billboard*, May 21, 2017. www.billboard.com/music/awards/bts-video-top-social-artist-win-billboard-music-awards-2017-7801216/.

Lucas, Sydney. "ARMYs Congratulate BTS's Jimin after He Earns an Honorary Diploma from Busan High School of Arts." *Koreaboo*, February 9, 2022. www.koreaboo.com/news/bts-jimin-honorary-diploma-busan-high-school-arts/.

Lukman, Josa. "Mihawk Back: The Dance Master of K-Pop Stars." *The Jakarta Post*, December 4, 2019. www.thejakartapost.com/life/2019/12/04/mihawk-back-the-dance-master-of-k-pop-stars.html.

McIntyre, Hugh. "BTS's 'Map of the Soul: 7' Is Now the Bestselling Album in South Korean History." *Forbes*, March 12, 2020. www.forbes.com/sites/hughmcintyre/2020/03/12/btss-map-of-the-soul-7-is-now-the-bestselling-album-in-south-korean-history/.

Melon. "2013 Melon Music Awards." 2013. www.melon.com/mma/result.htm?mmaYear=2013.

Pitchfork. "BTS Break Down Their Albums, from 'Dark & Wild' to 'Map of the Soul: 7.'" October 5, 2020. Interview video, 20:09. https://youtu.be/Tt9x61AL50E.

Tubiera, Alecsandra. "When BTS Members Donate to Charity They Inspire Fans to Do the Same." *South China Morning Post*, December 11, 2020. www.scmp.com/magazines/style/celebrity/article/3113575/when-bts-members-donate-charity-they-inspire-fans-do-same.

Yang, Haley. "Big Hit to Change Its Name to HYBE." *Korea JoongAng Daily*, March 11, 2021. https://koreajoongangdaily.joins.com/2021/03/11/entertainment/kpop/big-hit-entertainment-BTS-Bang-Sihyuk/20210311102700732.html.

Yeung, Jessie. "K-Pop Band BTS Earn Their First Grammy Nomination for Hit Song 'Dynamite.'" *CNN*, November 24, 2020. www.cnn.com/2020/11/24/entertainment/bts-grammy-nomination-intl-hnk-scli/index.html.

Yonhap News Agency. "Bangtan Boys Second EP 'Wings' Tops 8 Music Charts." October 11, 2016. https://en.yna.co.kr/view/AEN20161011003400315.

Yonhap News Agency. "BTS Becomes Bestselling K-Pop Singers." April 9, 2020. https://en.yna.co.kr/view/AEN20200409005900315.

Yonhap News Agency. "BTS Becomes First K-Pop Act to Perform at Grammys." January 27, 2020. https://en.yna.co.kr/view/AEN20200127003351315.

ABOUT THE AUTHOR

YERIN KIM is a pop culture and style editor based in New York City. Originally from Seoul and a graduate of Syracuse University's Newhouse School of Public Communications, she is passionate about spreading cultural sensitivity through the lens of entertainment, beauty, and fashion. Her writing has appeared in *PopSugar*, *Seventeen*, *InStyle*, and more. Notable works include a viral profile on Olympic gymnast Suni Lee and her catapult into fame, along with *PopSugar*'s first-ever Asian Pacific Islander American destination, among various stories dedicated to inclusivity.

THE ULTIMATE SWIFTIE EXPERIENCE!

Pick Up Your Copy Today!